# LINGHOLM

## Its Story and Memories

by Marjorie Dymock

# DEDICATION

This book is dedicated with love and gratitude
to my sister Joan
and in memory of our mother;
they both loved Lingholm

Published by Marjorie Dymock 2015
Colour photographs by author
Designed and Printed by McKanes Printers, Keswick  t: 017687 80574
ISBN No. 978-0-9933980-0-1
Price £9.50

# INTRODUCTION

This book is intended to tell the story of Lingholm as seen through recollections passed on to me, and from my own knowledge and memories of over thirty years from 1963 living and working there.

To many people the name Lingholm means only two things – beautiful and peaceful gardens on the western shore of Derwentwater and its association with Beatrix Potter. But Lingholm was more than that, it was a family home, at the heart of a country estate with tenanted farms and houses, and mixed woodland, all covering a total of one thousand acres, located in the tranquil Newlands valley. It was, however, no longer a working community of estate staff after reorganisation of the estate following the death of John, 1st Viscount Rochdale, in 1993, and the closure of the gardens after the death of Elinor, Viscountess Rochdale, in 1997.

Lingholm and the Rochdale family have been part of the Keswick and the wider Cumbrian community for almost the whole of the twentieth century and the early years of the twenty-first century, but the contribution made by Viscount Rochdale to the life and times of this country is not widely known and is surely worthy of recording for posterity.

During the years when his industrial and business life took him away regularly from Keswick he always kept in touch with Lingholm, and was never happier than when he arrived back in his Cumbrian home.

The stories of John, Viscount Rochdale, Lingholm gardens and estate in the last century are inextricably linked, and in the following pages I shall endeavour to give the reader a glimpse of an era that has gone but I hope will not be forgotten.

# CONTENTS

ACKNOWLEDGEMENTS

AUTHOR'S NOTE

INTRODUCTION

# ACKNOWLEDGEMENTS

I would like to thank the following for their help: Keith Richardson for his advice on reading the text of my book; John Cawood of the Beatrix Potter Society for his comments on the Beatrix Potter section of Chapter 4; The Guardian for permission to quote, at the beginning of Chapter 4, Mrs. Enid Wilson's "Country Diary" of 11th May 1970; Macmillan Estates and copyright Harold Macmillan for permission to quote from his memoirs; Cumbria Life for permission to use the photograph of David Imrie; and the Keswick Reminder for allowing the use of Viscount Rochdale's photograph from May 1993, and for an extract about Lingholm from Stuart Cresswell's column "Keswick 125 years ago" in 2011. Finally, thanks to my sister Joan for her poem at the end of the book, taken from her collection "Live Shadows" published in 1999.

# AUTHOR'S NOTE

While completing this book, two family bereavements have occurred: St. John, 2nd Viscount Rochdale, sadly passed away on 27th February, 2015, and his younger son, Christopher, sadly on 25th February, 2015. Also, John, 1st Viscount Rochdale's wartime batman, Alec Davidson, sadly died on 12th January, 2015, aged 99. Lastly, Sir Nicholas Winton, referred to on page 40, sadly died on 1st July, 2015 at the grand age of 106.

# CHAPTER ONE

*John, Viscount Rochdale:*
*Early family history – Own early life – War service –*
*Career and House of Lords – Cumbrian interests –*
*More family history – Social events – Completion of family story*

The story of Lingholm began in the 1870s, when it was built for Colonel J. F. Greenall of the well-known brewing family as a country retreat, to the design of the eminent Victorian architect Alfred Waterhouse, following his own individual 'modern' Gothic style; he had likewise already designed nearby Fawe Park and Rosetrees. He was of national renown, with the Natural History Museum, Manchester Town Hall, and many other public buildings throughout Britain to his credit.

In the early 1900s a certain Colonel George Kemp (later Baron Rochdale) decided to buy a home in the Lake District. His choice was Lingholm on the western shore of Derwentwater, and this was to be the family home. His father had visited the Lake District as early as 1840, so the connection with the area was to be maintained.

During the late 1890s Lingholm was sometimes unoccupied, but also let out as a summer holiday home, among the visitors being Beatrix Potter and her family, who spent several summers there. The surrounding woods were the perfect setting for Beatrix's artistic talents, and many scenes were depicted in her children's books.

George Kemp was chairman of his family firm, Kelsall & Kemp, woollen manufacturers, in Rochdale, and at the time he acquired Lingholm was Liberal MP for the Heywood Division of Manchester. In the 1906 general election he lost his parliamentary seat to Winston Churchill, but regained it in 1910. He had served in the Boer War, and in the First World War commanded 1/6 Battalion Lancashire Fusiliers, followed by command of two brigades in the 42nd Division, serving in the infamous 1915 Gallipoli campaign. He was so distressed by events there that he asked for special leave to return home to report the true facts of the devastating situation to the Prime Minister and General Kitchener. On his return to Gallipoli he became ill and was repatriated shortly before the final evacuation.

By the end of the First World War, Colonel Sir George Kemp (he was knighted in 1909 for political services) had been elevated to the peerage as Baron Rochdale, and son John, born in Rochdale in 1906, was at preparatory school at Sunningdale in Berkshire. John's childhood home remained either in Rochdale or his father's London home at The Old Hall, Highgate, though holidays were mostly spent at Lingholm. John went on to Eton – they were happy days – followed by entry to Trinity College Cambridge, where he took a Natural Sciences Tripos. His father had been to Shrewsbury, Balliol College Oxford, and Trinity College Cambridge, taking a Classical Tripos. Classics were obviously in his blood, as John studied both Latin and Greek at Eton.

A fond recollection of his Cambridge days was of his tutor, Tressilian Nicholas, a geologist, a kind and enthusiastic man, who had imparted that same enthusiasm to his student. He stayed with John at Lingholm in the long vacation of 1927. Many years later, John met Tressilian (then aged 100) at a Trinity reunion dinner. He recalled that earlier occasion, having admired John's driving skills on the journey up from Cambridge, reaching Lingholm in record time!

On leaving Cambridge in 1928 John Kemp joined the family firm, Kelsall & Kemp Ltd., woollen manufacturers in Rochdale. He started work on the shop floor, learning every process in the manufacture of woollen cloth, and worked his way up, eventually becoming chairman of the company after the death of his father in 1945.

In his early working life he would spend every weekend at Lingholm, travelling north in his favourite Bentley – he always had a passion for cars and knew intimately how they worked.

The foundation of the company was laid in 1815 by his great-grandfather, Henry Kelsall, whose daughter Emily married John's grandfather, George Tawke Kemp, thus bringing the two families together. By the end of the eighteenth century Rochdale had become the centre of the Lancashire woollen industry; when cotton had begun to play a large part in the life of the county, wool had moved to east Lancashire. Thus Kelsall & Kemp was established in Rochdale as an important woollen company, importing its raw material mainly from Australia, but also from New Zealand, South Africa and the Falkland Islands. In Australia a subsidiary company was formed in the early 1920s based in Launceston, Tasmania. When Kelsall & Kemp celebrated its 150th anniversary in 1965, its ninth subsidiary company had been established only two years before, so concentrating the individual processes of cloth production in each of these subsidiaries. During both World Wars the company was working to full capacity making vast quantities of shirting cloth for the armed forces; it was also well known for its flannel cloth, including the well-advertised 'Doctor Flannel.'

Kelsall & Kemp, like other companies, had to adapt to changing fashions, including the introduction of man-made fibres. So when in the 1980s onwards mergers began to take place, the company, having merged with another firm in the group, was taken over by West Riding Worsted & Woollen Mills, which in turn was eventually absorbed into the multinational Coats Paton, later Coats Viyella, and now Coats.

In 1931 John married Elinor Pease, daughter of Captain Ernest Pease of Darlington, whose ancestors were connected with the building of the Stockton-Darlington railway. Elinor was not unfamiliar with Cumbria, as her uncle (Ernest's brother) had been a great friend of John's father, and of the Vane family at Hutton-in-the-Forest; Willie Vane, a life-long friend, later became Lord Inglewood. During her young days she had spent many happy hours on family visits to Lingholm and Hutton.

Their early married life was spent at Helmshore, Rawtenstall, near the family firm in Rochdale, and life was secure and happy. John had learnt to fly and gained his pilot's licence in the mid-1930s, keeping his plane at Barton aerodrome in Lancashire. He sometimes flew up to Lingholm after finishing work on Saturdays (after a $5^{1}/_{2}$ day working week in those days!). A visitor from Rochdale once recalled that everyone knew John Kemp's plane, and that they could almost set their watches on a Saturday when he flew over on his way north to Keswick! A field between Keswick and Braithwaite on Lingholm land was the landing strip, and the plane with folding wings was kept in a wooden hut – still there to this day, and now used as a farming implement shed. Holiday visits to Switzerland gave him further flying experience, and his log book of these journeys remained among his life-long possessions.

As mentioned earlier, in 1928 John joined the family firm Kelsall & Kemp, which had recently established a branch in Tasmania. It was in 1936 that he and Elinor paid their first visit to that company, and had the experience of flying out to Australia by Imperial Airways, the forerunner of BOAC and now British Airways, taking several days with stopovers en route, and including travel by flying boat. Later trips 'down under' were undertaken in 1965 and 1970, the latter including America and Japan where port visits connected with his later Government Inquiry were also on the itinerary.

The 1930s moved to a close, and war loomed ever nearer. Having been a cadet at Eton, and in the Cambridge OTC, John joined the Workington TA Battery (Royal Artillery) in 1927 before he left university. He had always wanted to be a regular soldier, but his father encouraged him to join the family firm. This was a decision he never regretted, especially in view of his love of engineering and all things mechanical, and the wider horizons that later opened up to him. He was also going to get all the soldiering experience he would want in the years to come.

On the declaration of war, Major Kemp joined the 42nd East Lancashire Division (including the Border Regiment) and eventually went to France. In May 1940, with thousands of others in the British Expeditionary Force, he arrived on the beaches near Dunkirk to await rescue by the 'little ships.' Dunkirk harbour itself was described as a "smoking flaming hell of screaming Stukas and artillery fire." So, from beaches north and south of Dunkirk they waded out to the small boats waiting off shore. On May 21st Major Kemp managed to board a rowing boat, packed with twenty men and only two oars, and was told there was no more room. However, he happened to be at the front of the boat when he suddenly saw his batman in the water, and successfully pleaded for him to be pulled into the boat. Running the gauntlet of ever-present bombing, they made it to the crowded destroyer HMS Scimitar, which then had to continue taking evasive action across the Channel to England. Major Kemp's batman had worked for his father at Lingholm since 1936; after the war he returned to work at Lingholm until he left in 1953. Alec Davidson lived in Keswick until his death in January 2015, and always vowed that Major Kemp saved his life.

Following a short leave, the division was re-formed, and among several UK postings were Combined Operations at Inverary, and training at Army Staff College. This training, along with Combined Operations, prepared Major Kemp for his later war service when he was promoted to colonel and attached, with a Royal Navy friend, to the American forces in the Pacific in the war against Japan. A recollection concerning this same friend was that of his command of HMS Kipling, damaged in the stormy Battle of Crete in 1941. During that battle a sister ship, HMS Kelly, was sunk and, though crippled, the commander of Kipling turned his ship around and went to the rescue of Captain Lord Louis Mountbatten and his crew. His friend subsequently won a double DSO and Lord Mountbatten later went on to join the Pacific campaign.

Another recollection is that of Colonel Kemp's great friend from Cambridge days and best man at his wedding, David Nichol, who was lost at sea. He was on his way out to a posting with the UK Army Liaison Mission in Australia on the cargo and passenger liner 'Ceramic,' carrying military personnel and civilians, including women and children. Well out in the Atlantic, without any warning it was suddenly hit by a torpedo and sank with the loss of all 650 lives, except for one soldier who was picked up by the u-boat and taken prisoner.

Further poignant memories are of the later war years. Having arrived in the South Pacific, the intention was to help in plans for the recapture of Singapore. With others, Colonel Kemp was flown in a Dakota from Cairns, Northern Queensland to Lae in northern New Guinea. An American jeep then took them to a very small encampment on the shores of eastern New Guinea. With much apprehension as to what the coming days had in store, they felt very lonely and far from home. It was a Sunday evening, and someone had turned on a small radio; suddenly over the airwaves came the singing of a favourite hymn "The day thou gavest Lord is ended." The words "The sun that bids us rest is waking Our brethren 'neath the western sky" had such meaning at that moment; homesickness came flooding in along with boyhood memories of attending Crosthwaite Church with his parents, when Canon Hardwicke Rawnsley was the preacher.

Later in the Philippines at an Allied base camp, with the sound of Japanese gunfire all around, Colonel Kemp was sitting at a table with fellow officers, when the one next to him suddenly fell forward, cut down by a Japanese shell; he said he felt 'there but for the grace of God . . .'

He vividly remembered standing on the shore of Leyte Island in the Philippines with the welcoming party in October 1944 when General Douglas MacArthur, accompanied by the exiled Philippine President, waded ashore to fulfil his promise to the people that 'I shall return.' This recollection came to mind on seeing a photograph of the event in a book on the history of the Second World War, and saying 'I was there.' The Allied forces had fled the islands in 1942, overrun by the Japanese, and General MacArthur's return signalled the beginning of the end of the war in the Pacific.

In the later phase of the war, Colonel Kemp was promoted to temporary Brigadier, mentioned in despatches, and was awarded the OBE (Military Division) in 1945. Later he was awarded the long-service Territorial Decoration.

During both world wars Lingholm house played a not unimportant part. In the First World War from 1916 it was a convalescent military hospital run by staff of the Voluntary Aid Detachment (VADs) from Keswick with the aid of a local doctor and other helpers. Once, in the course of an underground repair in front of the house, a manhole cover was removed to reveal white tiles lining the sides of the drains – evidence of the existence of a hospital.

When the war was over, as a 'thank you' to the people of Keswick, the staff and patients got together and put on a variety programme in the Pavilion (now Riverside Lodge flats), ending with Elgar's 'Land of Hope and Glory.' Young John Kemp was there – it was remembered by him in later years with some nostalgia.

The Second World War saw Lingholm as a home for evacuee children from the north-east, among whom were a number of Austrian refugee children, with Lady Rochdale (John Kemp's mother) very much in charge. One day the office door bell rang, and there stood a lady who had come to see again the home where she had once found refuge; she so enjoyed wandering round the grounds and reliving her childhood memories.

In March 1945, as the war in Europe was nearing its end, Baron Rochdale died, and John Kemp inherited his father's title. It was to be some months before he returned from the Far East to civilian life and saw his wife and young son, St. John, then aged seven. Elinor had, in fact, joined the ATS for about two years, becoming a chief Commandant, and based in the UK.

On returning to Britain after the war, Lord Rochdale eventually moved to Lingholm to live. The place he had loved since childhood now became his home, and in future years would become a peaceful haven in his active business life.

He soon took his seat in the House of Lords and attended whenever the demands of his other work allowed. As chairman he was very much involved in his own family textile firm, and in later years became deputy chairman of the parent company, West Riding Worsted and Woollen Mills. He showed an interest in local matters from first settling in Cumberland, as it then was, and became a Deputy Lieutenant in 1947. Following his war service he re-formed and commanded the local TA Field Regiment of the Westmorland & Cumberland Yeomanry, and remained Hon. Colonel until its disbandment in 1967.

He became a member of the British Legion (later Royal British Legion) during his days in Rochdale, was President of the North West Area in the late 1950s and remained a staunch supporter all his life. In 1977 he took the salute at the Keswick War Memorial at the Dedication of the new Keswick Legion Standard. Throughout the years he attended regularly the annual Service of Remembrance in Keswick. What was quite unique was that he was always welcomed to the Service by another strong supporter of the Legion, Alec Davidson, his batman from the early war years.

Wider horizons, however, beckoned. His interest and ability in public affairs was soon recognised when in 1952 Lord Rochdale became a member of the Central Transport Consultative Committee. From then on he received further public appointments, a number of them connected with manufacturing industry. He was made President of the National Union of Manufacturers from 1953 to 1956, and later became a member of the Council of its successor, the Confederation of British Industry (CBI).

In the 1950s, through his knowledge of industrial and trade matters, he undertook a lecture tour of the USA and Canada under the auspices of the Foreign Office and Commonwealth Relations Office. During this period he was also appointed a governor of the BBC, and more industrial and bank appointments were taken up, continuing into the 1970s.

His expertise in the textile industry brought the prestigious appointment as Chairman of the Cotton Board in 1957. This came at a time when the Lancashire cotton industry was in decline because of competition from India, Pakistan and Hong Kong, and he was given the challenge of negotiating an agreement to limit exports of cheap goods from India and Pakistan. However, the stumbling block was Hong Kong, still a British territory, but visits to the colony eventually brought agreement and a limit to its exports. In his memoirs Harold Macmillan, Prime Minister at that time wrote: "The Chairman of the British Cotton Board was Lord Rochdale, a man of infinite patience and skill, combined with absolute integrity. Without Rochdale we could have achieved nothing. I never ceased to admire his devotion to a task which he had undertaken purely from a sense of public duty."

It was in the New Year's Honours of 1960 that Lord Rochdale was created a Viscount by Harold Macmillan in recognition of his achievements in the textile industry. He once said he felt he had now earned his title – it was his own – and had not just inherited it from his father.

Lord Rochdale's long-standing association with the textile world twice brought him the post of Upper Bailiff (Chairman) of the Worshipful Company of Weavers, one of the oldest of the City of London Livery Companies; he was also made a Companion Member of the Textile Institute (a worldwide organisation) in 1962, finally receiving the Institute Medal in 1986 at a ceremony in Manchester for his outstanding contribution to the textile industry.

Early in the 1960s another challenge presented itself when the Government asked Lord Rochdale to head a Committee of Inquiry into the Major Ports of Great Britain. This took him into a different industrial sphere, one which was to last for fifteen years. The committee produced the "Rochdale Report," recommending rationalisation and increased investment in the docks. As a result, in 1963 a National Ports Council was set up, based in London, and he became its first Chairman. Following four years in this post, he relinquished it when asked by the President of the Board of Trade to head an Inquiry to review the structure and organisation of the shipping industry; this involved considerable travel, and three years later in 1970 the second "Rochdale Report" was produced. Both reports became what were considered authoritative textbooks for their respective industries. During this period Lord Rochdale's right-wing political affiliation did not cause a problem for the then Labour Government; they thought highly of his abilities, and were only too glad to be able to call on his services.

Not to be daunted by the economic and political problems of the day, in 1971 he was offered and accepted the chairmanship of Belfast shipbuilders Harland & Wolff, an appointment by the Northern Ireland Government. In the heyday of the oceangoing liners, Harland & Wolff had built, among others, the Titanic and Queen Mary, but many cargo and other commercial carriers were to be built over the years. It also comprised other divisions dealing with ship repairing, engineering and electrical manufacturing. Lord Rochdale took over at a difficult time politically, in the early years of the troubles with the IRA. Although there were bomb threats to the shipyard, fortunately nothing worse happened, and his anti-sectarian leadership had a great influence on the harmony of the workforce. He took charge soon after a great modernisation programme had taken place, which had produced the largest shipbuilding dock and the largest crane (known as 'Goliath') in the world at that time, to cater for the building of VLCCs (very large crude carriers) of up to 300,000 tonnes. Although some of these giants had already been built and launched, the age of the supertanker was in fact coming to an end, and shipbuilding was changing. The company's viability became difficult to maintain and, although his term of office only had a few months to run, when the government stepped in to reconstruct the company in November 1975, he decided to resign.

Harland & Wolff asked Lord Rochdale to return in December of that year to give the prizes at the first formal presentation of technical awards, at which he donated the Rochdale Trophy to be competed for annually for the Best All-round Apprentice of the Year. During the same visit, at a presentation made to him, he bade farewell to the company.

This was to be his last major public appointment, and with these duties now behind him, he was able to concentrate more on his attendance at the House of Lords.

Lord Rochdale had always taken his responsibilities as a member of the House seriously, but also enjoyed the companionship of his fellow peers, some of whom he had known for many years. He was at prep school with Quinton Hogg, later Lord Hailsham and a Lord Chancellor in the Thatcher Government. When his long-time friend and Cumbrian neighbour, Willie Whitelaw, was created a Viscount in the 1980s, Lord Rochdale was one of the two peers who introduced him to the Lords. Lord Whitelaw had also become Secretary of State for Northern Ireland when the Government took over from Stormont. This was in the early days of Lord Rochdale's chairmanship of Harland & Wolff; they found themselves neighbours for a time in Belfast.

Although not a 'political animal,' Lord Rochdale enjoyed the Lords' debates and the civilised manner in which they were conducted, and attended as regularly as he could. Indeed, he nearly always responded to his Party's call if there was a three-line Whip, perhaps for a particularly important or controversial Bill, and the 600-mile journey by train to London and back, often by overnight sleeper, never seemed to daunt him, even in his later years.

He contributed to debates that were mainly within the area of his expertise: trade and industry, shipping and other transport matters. He had always held the view that universities should not always encourage students to enter the professions as a career to the exclusion of manufacturing industry, for so long thought of as 'dirty' work. He knew that the creation of wealth depended so much on the success of manufacturing industry, and the ability to trade worldwide; everything else would follow. He felt so strongly about this that in December 1978 he introduced his own Private Debate (a rare occurrence) on this subject, to encourage young people with the best brains to enter manufacturing industry as a career. He was commended for his speech by many people in the industrial and educational world and for the stand he had taken.

Continuing his activities in the Lords, in the 1980s Lord Rochdale became a member of the Select Committee on European Affairs. His expertise in industrial matters led him to chair the Sub-Committee on Trade and Industry, and the Reports produced by this and other sub-committees were regarded as authoritative and valuable documents.

Throughout his years in the business world, he had always realised that change was inevitable, and nothing could stand still. So it was with the House of Lords, where he had always believed that some reform was required; this had been on the agenda since earlier Reform Bills. Whether he would have approved of the sweeping changes undertaken by the Blair Government in gradually getting rid of the hereditary peers, and further changes yet to come, we shall never know. What is known, however, is that the House of Lords includes members, both hereditary and life peers, with a wealth of experience in many fields who could still be of great service to the government of the day.

The Rochdale family connection with Parliament goes back a long way, in that the first stone of the Clock Tower of the new Houses of Parliament was laid in 1843 by Lord Rochdale's grandmother, Emily Kelsall, before she married his grandfather. The engraved ceremonial trowel used on that occasion is kept in the Record Office at the Houses of Parliament. This event occurred through the friendship of Lord Rochdale's great-grandfather, Henry Kelsall, with Sir Samuel Morton Peto, the Victorian civil engineer, the creator of the Parliament building.

Although involved in the business world away from home, Lord Rochdale never lost his interest in Cumbrian and northern affairs. In 1974 he was made President of the North West Industrial Development Association, holding this post for ten years. This was a highly informed pressure group, non-party political, developed over a long time, which brought the problems of the North West to the attention of the then government; he was pleased that Cumbria had been brought into the fold.

When local rural affairs needed a focus, the Cumbria Rural Enterprise Agency was formed, and in 1986 he became a director, retiring from the post five years later.

He was passionate about preserving the Lake District as an area of natural beauty, and as Chairman of the Lake District Committee of the National Trust for many years, he was able to make his contribution. Likewise, his love of music brought him the chairmanship of Rosehill Arts Trust, Whitehaven, and he spent many happy evenings at concerts at Rosehill Theatre, founded by his good friend Sir Nicholas Sekers. He had also been keenly interested in ongoing efforts to establish a permanent theatre in Keswick, so how he would have loved to have seen and visited the Theatre by the Lake.

In the story of Lord Rochdale's life, only his father's side of the family had so far been mentioned. But his mother's family also has a very interesting history. She was Lady Beatrice Egerton, third daughter of the third Earl of Ellesmere, whose family home was Worsley Hall, near Manchester. Lord Rochdale remembered visits to his grandfather's home as a boy, and an early memory was of one occasion as a very small boy being lifted up so he could watch the arrival of King Edward VII on a visit to Worsley Hall.

During her earlier years Lady Beatrice Rochdale became a suffragist, the non-militant branch of the suffragettes, the movement being very strong in industrial Lancashire. When she came to live at Lingholm in the early 1900s, her earlier suffragist activities would most likely have brought her into contact with Catherine Marshall, keen local suffragist and next door neighbour at Hawes End. Lady Beatrice was at Lingholm in the First World War when it became a convalescent military hospital, and she became involved in public life in Keswick and Cumbria, notably the Red Cross and British Legion. As mentioned earlier, when Lingholm became a home for evacuees during the Second World War, she supervised their welfare.

The Ellesmere connection with Lancashire and Merseyside goes back a long way, in fact to an ancestor of the 18th century, Francis Egerton, the third Duke of Bridgewater, or the 'Canal Duke,' as he was known, and whose home, Bridgewater House, was near Runcorn on the River Mersey. He made his fortune through coal, but needed a cheap means of transporting it from his Worsley collieries to the centre of the cotton industry and its spinning mills in the Manchester area.

So the idea was born of building a canal over the 28 miles from Worsley to Manchester. He engaged the services of a mining engineer, James Brindley, who had previously worked on tunnelling projects in the Worsley coal mines. The building of the first modern canal in Britain, the Bridgewater Canal, commenced in 1759, was completed in 1765 at a cost of £50,000 and included the swing-bridge Barton aquaduct (still there to this day) over the Manchester Ship Canal. This engineering achievement heralded a new era, as more and more canals were built to become the arteries of the great new Industrial Revolution.

The Duke's name lives on in Bridgewater House in London, occupied by later generations of the Ellesmere family, including Lord Rochdale's grandfather. At that time it was the largest private non-royal residence in London but, like other such large houses, was later sold to a commercial company to cover death duties. This was the home where his cousins were brought up – Lady Margaret Egerton and her brother John, who succeeded a kinsman in 1963 to become the Duke of Sutherland. Lady

Margaret became a lady-in-waiting first to Princess Elizabeth, and then to the Queen Mother. She married Sir John Colville, private secretary to Princess Elizabeth, and later to Winston Churchill.

The Bridgewater name is remembered today in the new concert hall in Manchester, the Bridgewater Hall, now the home of the Hallé Orchestra, which vacated the Free Trade Hall some years ago for its now permanent home. In their early married life, John and Elinor regularly attended Hallé concerts there conducted by the legendary Sir Hamilton Harty. Lord Rochdale would have been highly delighted to know that the Hallé's new home was named after his pioneering ancestor.

Lord Rochdale's life story must of course include that of his wife Elinor, who entered fully into the life of the county and beyond. Mention has already been made of her younger days, from marriage in 1931, and her war service in the ATS.

However, following the end of the war, and her move to Lingholm after the death of Lord Rochdale's father, she gradually threw herself into both local and national affairs. She was a very independent person, and took an active part in various organisations, quite apart from her husband's work. She was very keen on politics and, as a staunch Conservative, became involved in the North-East Conservative Association – her family's home was originally in the Darlington area. In recognition of her political work, she was awarded the CBE in the 1960s.

In Cumbria in the 60s and 70s Elinor served in many voluntary bodies within the Cumberland Council of Social Service, and its successor Voluntary Action Cumbria, and on retirement in 1975 became Vice-President, then President, and finally Life President in 1989 to mark her 25 years' service. Rural affairs were also a passion, with service on the Rural Community Council for Cumbria, her work covering many social and community projects including housing and rural services. Elinor also served as secretary of the Cumbria Association of Local Councils, supporting rural developments in Furness and Allerdale. Other interests included the Guild of Lakeland Craftsmen and the Women's Institute, being a member of one of the local branches.

Elinor's love of music – she was an accomplished pianist – led to her being one of the original members of Keswick Music Society, formed in 1947. Later she was President for many years until 1985. Whenever she could she attended concerts, even when somewhat infirm in her later years. Along with her husband, she regularly attended concerts at Rosehill.

As President of the Cumbria branch of the NSPCC, for many years Elinor hosted an annual fundraising coffee morning at Lingholm – a very popular occasion for local people. Another most important interest was the Cumbria branch of the Victoria League for Commonwealth Friendship, later including other overseas nationalities, which she founded in the 1950s. Overseas students from Newcastle and Lancaster universities would spend a day in the Keswick area annually in the spring and autumn, given hospitality at a hotel lunch with local supporters, followed by a launch trip on Derwentwater, and tea with families in their homes, either in Keswick or Penrith. Quite a few friendships were forged during these years. Changing circumstances, however, brought about the demise of the Victoria League in 2006.

Elinor's legacy is the Calvert Trust Adventure Centre for the Disabled, of which she was a founder member with John Fryer Spedding in 1974. After much hard work the centre was opened in 1978 by the Duke of Buccleugh, wheelchair bound as the result of an accident. She devoted a great deal of time and effort in encouraging fundraising and watching the centre develop and grow, with visitors arriving from far and wide to enjoy the numerous outdoor and indoor activities. The Keswick centre was so successful that others were later opened at Kielder and Exmoor. Elinor was very optimistic and determined that all would succeed, and she became President of the Council of the three centres in 1995. Her one 'adventure' with Calvert, when very much in the autumn of her life, was to abseil down an 80ft. crag at Castlehead quarry.

Following the death of her husband in 1993, Elinor's life was totally dedicated to seeing that the gardens and tea room flourished, and she always hoped they would be enjoyed by locals and visitors for many years to come. Sadly, this was not to be, and they were closed early in 1997, soon after she passed away.

Although Lord and Lady Rochdale were very private people, they were always generous in their hospitality. Social and musical events were held in their home, both for their friends and local organisations. A special occasion was a reception for townspeople to celebrate the Queen's Silver Jubilee in 1977.

Over the years the grounds of Lingholm house were also the venue for a number of events. Two notable ones occurred in later years: one was a fundraising supper party in 1990 for the Army Benevolent Fund when the Border Regiment military band, on a fine early autumn evening, played on the lawn in front of the house. The other was a display of Classic Rolls

Royce cars, lined up in front of the house, during their enthusiasts' weekend tour through the Lake District in May 1991; they enjoyed morning coffee in the nearby gardens' tea room. These were particularly relevant in view of Lord Rochdale's life-long interest in the army and his love of cars.

Memories of Lord and Lady Rochdale would not be complete without remembering their daughter, Bryony. She was only sixteen in 1963 when she died three weeks after a bad fall during the school summer holidays while she and her mother were riding their ponies on the estate; her death was a great sadness for her parents and brother St. John. Later the delightful sunken garden at the main entrance to the gardens at Lingholm became a memorial to Bryony with beautifully crafted gates bearing her name and the animals that she loved. Two dove sculptures in her memory appear on the gate leading out of this garden.

Finally, one cannot bring the Rochdale family story to an end without mentioning their three families of Pekinese dogs – from the 1960s they were their faithful companions for the next thirty years.

*Victoria League overseas guests with hosts*

*Calvert Trust Opening April 1978 (Lady Rochdale on right)*

*Border Regiment Band on front lawn 1990*

15

*Classic Rolls Royce cars at front of house 1991*

*Bryony – Memorial Garden*

*Grandchildren in 1973 (Jonathan, now 3rd Viscount, Joanna, Susanna, and the late Christopher)*

16

*Brumas, Bridie, Winkle*

*Puffy, Honey*

*Brumas, Suki*

# CHAPTER TWO

*Estate: Early days – David Imrie, Gamekeeper – Forestry*

When Lord Rochdale inherited the Lingholm Estate in 1945, it covered a much larger area than in subsequent years. In the early part of last century the estate had been built up piecemeal and extended from Derwent Bog at the head of Bassenthwaite Lake to parts of Underskiddaw; Borrowdale, including Barrow House, Ashness and Watendlath; and part of the Newlands valley. Later the estate was confined to farms, houses and cottages, together with 400 acres of woodland, in the Newlands valley, totalling 1000 acres. In addition, in the early days, Lord Rochdale's father had secured sporting rights on certain local tracts of land, and on the Gunnerside estate in Swaledale – over 30,000 acres of fine grouse moorland – together with the house, Gunnerside Lodge.

The original planting of a wide variety of trees on much of the land on the western shore of Derwentwater was undertaken by the then owner, Lord William Gordon, in the late eighteenth century; he built Derwent Bay House as his home. After the death of Lady Gordon in 1834 her nephew, Major-General Sir John George Woodford, inherited the estate and lived in Derwent Bay House until his death in 1879. Neither of these owners wished to fell any trees, but some felling did take place much later in the First World War as a contribution to the war effort. Lord Rochdale's father created further plantations, mostly on Swinside, near Little Braithwaite, and in the Newlands valley, all in the interest of a spectacular pheasant shoot; together with the Gunnerside shoots they constituted a considerable part of life on the Lingholm estate.

Those early years were a world away from that of today. Life was lived at a slower pace, and landowners could afford the outlay necessary to enable them to enjoy weekend shoots with invited guests. This was the heyday of the gamekeeper, and in the mid-1920s a young Scot from near Aberdeen, David Imrie, arrived to take up his duties as gamekeeper on the estate, where he worked for the next fifty years. His home was a simple hut in the Braithwaite woods at the edge of the Newlands valley, with no electricity or running water. He had to walk 100 yards to a water tap at the entrance gate to the wood; he cooked on an open fire in an old-fashioned blackleaded grate, and had only paraffin lamps for lighting.

This was the life he liked; he was a 'loner,' solitary but never lonely. He guarded his privacy, and rarely if ever could anyone step over the threshold of his hut. He was a man who lived close to nature, and what he didn't know about the wildlife around him wasn't worth knowing. He was a man of many parts: a talented artist, with nature and landscapes as his subjects, a self-taught linguist, a writer of both poetry and prose, a regular contributor for twenty-five years to The Shooting Times, and author of 'Lakeland Gamekeeper,' published in 1949, but no longer in print. Following in his father's footsteps, he had learned to play the bagpipes as a teenager, and he continued this throughout his life. It is said that on fine summer evenings the sound of his playing could be heard down in Braithwaite village.

*David Imrie – early days*

When David worked for Lord Rochdale's father he was one of a team of four keepers, with other help provided on a part-time basis. In the 1920s some thousands of pheasants were reared each year for the weekend shooting parties, the season beginning in November. The parties, no more than eight people, were guests in the house, arriving on Friday evening and returning home on Monday evening. Game dealers marketed the pheasants further afield, and each estate farmer, tenant and keeper received a brace as a token of goodwill.

From 1936 for eight seasons David helped with shooting parties on the grouse moors of Swaledale, based at Gunnerside Lodge. He would go out on each occasion to load for his employer who, even though latterly quite lame, would be taken out to the butts in a sledge drawn by a pony. At Lingholm during the Second World War timber from the Swinside woodlands was felled for the war effort; pheasant shoots were gradually coming to a close, and David's world of gamekeeping was now to change radically.

In the early days of the forestry operations, there had been a serious countrywide rabbit problem, which was overcome with the help of a government assisted Rabbit Clearance Society, the local one being for Above Derwent. David, no longer a gamekeeper, and not yet ready to retire, took on the job as vermin destroyer for the Society. It so happened that myxomatosis affected rabbits at that time and, although a terrible affliction, shortened the period of constant surveillance of newly planted areas of woodland. David continued until retirement keeping moles and rabbits at bay on farmland and in the gardens, and he tracked roe deer that wandered the woods often destroying young trees. Tree guards were then used more and more, and after David's retirement a member of the forestry department kept watch. Later a stalker was employed on a casual basis, culling any sick or injured deer.

When he retired David made a farewell appearance at the staff Christmas party by playing the bagpipes, the first time anyone there had heard him play. He left his hut in the woods (later taken over as the local base for a Lancashire mountaineering club), and found home comforts in a small cottage in Braithwaite surrounded by his paintings and books. Neighbours kept an eye on him until he had to go into care; he died in late October 1985. On a sunny crisp autumn day old friends attended his funeral at Newlands church, at which Lord Rochdale gave the address. David was laid to rest in the churchyard there in his beloved Newlands valley.

The end of the Second World War, and the death of Lord Rochdale's father, inevitably brought changes to the estate. Regular shoots had already come to an end, and the Swaledale grouse moors sold off. There had been unavoidable wartime neglect of the woods, and it therefore now seemed right to establish a forestry department with a proper management policy; this became an important element in the Lingholm estate operations.

The main woodlands covered 400 acres in the Newlands valley surrounding the estate farm land, and included the Home Woods nearer Lingholm house. Five-year plans for management of the woods were produced with the help of the Forestry Commission and a forestry adviser, and useful government forestry grants became available.

Commercial interests demanded the planting of fast-growing conifers, but with the already well-established broadleaved trees the woodlands, now being maintained on a regular basis, enhanced the local landscape. Adverse comments have been made about the angular blocks of conifer plantations that have sprung up over the years throughout the country, and the estate took this fact into consideration with plantings that were more visually pleasing. Forestry is obviously a long-term enterprise – some conifers can take up to twenty-five years to mature – so planning is all-important, with a policy of regular planting, thinning and felling.

The forestry department gradually developed into a self-sufficient unit, fully mechanised, and able to supply timber to a ready market. Conifers were converted into fencing posts for local farmers, into pulpwood for the paper industry, and pallet wood for numerous industrial uses. Large timber felled was a mixture of both hardwood and softwood, collected from the roadside by forestry contractors. This was the pattern for the next forty years.

An offshoot of timber production at Lingholm was the supply of hardwood logs, offcuts from fellings, to both local residents and visitors, especially as holiday homes sprang up and the use of woodburning stoves became more popular. The logs were normally delivered by tractor and trailer, and had a wide distribution. However, as Lingholm logs became more popular, it was necessary to restrict sales to a smaller catchment area. It was very time consuming, took the foresters away from mainstream forestry operations, and later inevitably had to cease.

For many years Lingholm supplied Christmas trees to local people. They were always cut freshly every day, stacked in the yard outside the estate office, and collected from there. One especially large one was always delivered to the house a few days before Christmas, and became the centrepiece of the staff Christmas party. In later years, however, the relatively small number of trees ordered made this operation no longer viable, and it also unfortunately had to cease.

It was the policy of the estate as an employer to help young people to gain practical experience in various ways. The National Forestry School at Newton Rigg near Penrith often recommended students to apply to Lingholm estate for their one year's pre-college training before proceeding to their diploma courses. This was also beneficial to the forestry department, where extra help was always welcome. Small student groups would sometimes spend time at Lingholm on various projects, and final year students on one occasion in the late 1980s undertook a detailed survey of estate forestry, resulting in one of the most comprehensive reports ever produced, making a valuable contribution to future estate forestry policy. World supplies of timber were expected to increasingly diminish, with UK timber supplies in greater demand from private estates as well as from Forestry Commission woodlands.

In periods of prolonged dry weather, the risk of fire was ever present and fire hazard notices warned the public of this. However, one evening in the summer of 1989, flames were seen in the conifer plantation on top of Swinside fell. Fire engines were quickly on the scene and the firemen, with the willing help of estate staff, worked through the night to contain and extinguish the fire within a small section of the fell top. The cause of the fire was believed to be an empty glass bottle caught by the sun; fortunately not too many trees were lost.

By contrast, two years earlier in 1987 a very different scenario occurred when a devastating hurricane in October struck the south of England. Newick Park, a private home and conference centre in East Sussex, with an area of 240 acres of beautifully landscaped parkland and woodland garden, was severely hit, losing many huge and old trees, some rare specimens of historical and landscape value. The owners of Newick, friends of the Rochdale family, did not have specialised forestry staff or equipment, so arrangements were made for the Lingholm team to travel to Sussex to help clear the debris. They stayed for some days, and as a result of their hard work Newick was able to open to the public the following spring.

The Prince of Wales became President of the Royal Forestry Society in the 1980s, and inaugurated the Duke of Cornwall's Award for Forestry and Conservation, to encourage owners of mainly commercial woodlands to manage them in sympathy with the landscape and wildlife conservation. To be competed for by the regions, in 1989 it was the turn of the North of England, and Lingholm was encouraged to enter the competition. The RFS awarded first prize to Low Fell, Grizedale Forest (Forestry Commission), and joint second prizes, one to Lingholm, the only privately owned woods, and the other to Dalby Forest, North Yorkshire, another Forestry Commission woodland. Lingholm's award, a medallion and certificate of merit, was received by Lord Rochdale's son, St. John Kemp, and Ronnie Pepper, head forester, at the Great Yorkshire Show, Harrogate by the then Minister of Agriculture.

Lingholm forestry department had attracted the attention of the Royal Forestry Society for its successful management of its woodlands, and in

1989 an Open Day was held for members in the northern region. They were taken out to the woods to see first hand foresters at work.

A similar event was held in the early 1980s for members of the local Country Landowners' Association, when forestry operations were demonstrated in the forestry yard at Derwent Bay.

After a distinguished career of over thirty years with the Forestry Commission, Alan Mitchell, an internationally acclaimed tree expert, retired in 1984. As author of 'Trees of Great Britain' and other publications, he had travelled round Britain and Ireland collecting information on the best and largest specimen trees. He kept ongoing records of these trees, and noted a Norway spruce (the true Christmas tree) at Lingholm in 1992, 145 feet tall with a girth of 16 feet, as the "inheritor of the title of best specimen. It stands in the middle of a broad path through beech and pine woods, and can be seen in all its majesty."

*CLA Open Day*

# Spring – *formal garden area*

# Spring – *woodland garden*

*Lord Rochdale in his woodland garden April 1993*

# Autumn – *house and grounds*

# Winter wonderland

# CHAPTER THREE

*Lingholm house – Estate community: Farms – Staff –*
*Social occasions*

Like most country estates the way of life in the 'big house' before
the Second World War was one that no longer exists. There were about a
dozen staff, including butler, cook, housekeeper, lady's maid, housemaids,
footmen and chauffeur, with staff quarters on the top floor of the house,
and a sitting room on the ground floor, which later became the library.
This room had high windows and window sills, which was apparently to
deter staff from looking outside, or maybe being seen to do so! In those
days the house had an extra wing with an impressive porte cochère at the
front door, both of which were demolished in the 1950s in the interests of
economy.

It was quite usual for the 'big house' to include a small chapel, and
this was so at Lingholm. In the early days staff were encouraged to attend
Sunday evening prayers, with the vicar of Crosthwaite Church taking
the service once a month. The chapel was later converted into the estate
office in the 1950s.

The main rooms of the house are very impressive, including the entrance
hall and staircase, with oak floors and panelling throughout. Unusually,
gilded leather panelling covered the walls of the entrance hall, dominated
by an intricately carved oak fireplace with Corinthian columns. On either
side of the fireplace blue velvet covered chairs occupied by the Rochdales
at the Queen's Coronation in 1953 took pride of place; all who attended
were allowed to keep the chairs. The large Stone room, known as such
because of the Lakeland slate walls built above lower half oak panelling,
also has a huge beautifully carved stone fireplace. This is said to date
from the early 15th century, to have come from a palace in Tuscany, and
to have been bought in Florence in 1903. The dining room has oak
panelling and a magnificent James I carved oak fireplace (the royal coat
of arms is clearly shown), originally in a royal house in Southampton,
and acquired by Lord Rochdale's father when he was planning changes
in the interior of Lingholm. It is understood that the house was destroyed
in the bombing during the Second World War; the fine panelling had,
therefore, been saved for posterity.

Lord Rochdale's father furnished Lingholm with collections of early
English and Continental oak and walnut furniture. Other collections

included 16th and 17th century Flemish tapestries, 16th century Italian majolica, silver and glassware.

Work in the house, recalled by Alec Davidson, who was handyman before the war, included beeswaxing the floors in the main rooms, and rising early to light the coke-fired boilers, the fuel being delivered then by horse and cart. Alec met his wife at Lingholm while she was working as a kitchen maid.

Alec had joined the Territorial Army before the war and was called up for service in 1939. After demobilisation in 1945 he went to work temporarily in the Rochdales' Lancashire home before they moved to Lingholm the following year. There Alec resumed his various estate duties while his wife worked as cook in the house. He remained until 1953 when he left to take up other employment. Another husband and wife partnership, Jack and Margaret Woods, arrived from Lancashire in 1946; their daughter Della is still living in Keswick to this day.

On the arrival of Lord and Lady Rochdale at Lingholm there were inevitable reductions in house staff. However, a cook/housekeeper, chauffeur/handyman, and two or three part-time staff were taken on, with accommodation provided both in the house and in other nearby cottages. Two flats on the top floor of the house were originally occupied by staff, and later became holiday flats; two further flats accommodated house staff and personal secretary.

Moving away from the house and its environs, the estate land comprised forestry compartments of 400 acres surrounding several tenanted farms and houses in the Newlands valley. Skelgill farm nestled under Catbells, the furthest estate farm higher up the valley, with Swinside farm next door, Ullock farm (originally two smaller farms, Ullock and Ullock Grange) further down the valley, Uzzicar farm on the other side of Newlands under Barrow fell, and near old copper mine workings, and Little Braithwaite farm on the edge of Braithwaite village.

These were upland sheep and dairy farms, including beef cattle at one time. Some farms included a flock of traditional Herdwick sheep, and when a tenancy ended the new tenant automatically inherited that flock, called 'heafed,' i.e. the sheep knew and kept to the land on which they were reared. Gradually Swaledale and other breeds were introduced.

They were family farms, some passed down from father to son. In the early days nearby houses and cottages were occupied by a farm worker, but when no longer required as such, were let to outside tenants. When a tenancy ended, in a few cases it made sense to sell the property.

In the early 1960s the estate farms benefited from government hill farming scheme grants then in operation. Subsequently, changing times brought about other government grants to help farmers adapt and diversify and, as with many farms elsewhere, a bed and breakfast business often supplemented the farm income. Readers will probably be surprised to learn that it was only in the early 1960s that the Newlands valley was eventually completely linked to mains electricity.

School and scout camps were often accommodated on land at Ullock and Little Braithwaite farms during school holidays; this was also a welcome source of income for the farmers. In fact, one school from the north-east of England returned regularly to Ullock farm for nearly twenty years.

Properties, of course, need maintaining, and so a maintenance department had been established on the estate to look after repairs and renovations. The workshop was based at Derwent Bay (or Waterend, as it was known in earlier days), together with a group of several properties, situated on the shore of the lake about a mile further south from Lingholm house. Derwent Bay House, the largest and oldest of the houses, was the home of the owner of the estate who lived there in the 19th century. After his death in 1879, as far as is known, it remained empty for many years, but much later was used as a workshop and store for materials until the main house was finally refurbished and, with a small flat conversion for estate staff, occupied by tenants.

When a new foreman and craftsman joiner, Joe Grave, joined the maintenance department in 1951, he lived at Derwent Bay. Other estate staff, as well as outside tenants, were housed nearby. Next door to the estate workshop was the forestry building where timber was prepared for sale; circular saws and creosoting plant were often in use. With tractors and other vehicles coming and going to both workshop and forestry yard, Derwent Bay became quite a hive of activity. Following Joe Grave's retirement in the early 1980s, Paul Bullock, a local man, became maintenance foreman for the next few years. A new foreman, Terry Wood, after completing his army career, came from Lancashire in 1989 and lived at Uzzicar farmhouse, remaining for the next six years until he left in 1995 following reorganisation of the estate.

In 1983 Lord Rochdale's son, St. John Kemp, joined the 'family firm' and came to live next door to Lingholm at Rosetrees. After gaining experience in the various estate departments, he took a course on Upland Farming at Newton Rigg College.

When the tenant farmers at Uzzicar and Skelgill retired about then, St. John became farm manager for Lingholm Farms, a new department of the estate. The land of both farms was taken over as one enterprise complete with their flocks of sheep, and a shepherd and family installed in Skelgill farmhouse.

The estate, as a busy commercial enterprise, was an important provider of employment in Keswick. Over the years members of many local families were employed at Lingholm, in forestry, gardens and maintenance, whether on a short or long-term basis. Others had come to live in the area and were looking for work; some were trainees en route to higher education in their field. Each department employed up to a maximum of four staff, including those on a Young Workers' Scheme and a Youth Training Scheme in the 1970s, and on a continuing basis in gardens and forestry in pre-college practical training.

A few staff, of course, were more established in their careers and were looking for long-term employment. Such was the case with the head gardener, Sidney Harrison, who came from Yorkshire in 1950, lived at The Lodge, and worked for over thirty years until retirement. Joe Grave, maintenance foreman, arrived in 1951 from West Cumbria, and also completed over thirty years' service before he retired. Both Sidney and Joe remained in their homes on retirement. Head forester Ronnie Pepper, from a Keswick family, came in 1964 as a trainee to work under the then head forester, Eddie McVittie. On the latter's departure a few years later, Ronnie was appointed to succeed him and remained working at Lingholm until reorganisation, having also completed thirty years' service. Sadly, he passed away prematurely in 2012.

Long service was also true of the house staff. The earlier 'live-in' cook/housekeeper Ethel Hall, and Tom McGowan chauffeur, who lived nearby, both arrived in the 1950s. Before retiring they found their own homes in Keswick, worked part-time for a short while, and finally completed thirty years at Lingholm.

It was now necessary to engage another couple as soon as possible, occupying a flat in the house. In 1989 Brian and Jessie Tustain, who had arrived back in the UK after working in America, were taken on. After Brian's sudden sad death a year later, Jessie remained until early 1991. In the meantime Maureen and Tony Jones had arrived and took up their duties in the house; they had returned to the UK from New Zealand, and remained after Lord Rochdale's death in 1993.

When possible estate staff were given 'tied' accommodation. During the 1960s and 1970s, however, Keswick residents would occasionally provide lodgings for single people arriving to take up employment, and the estate was able to help in finding suitable accommodation. As times changed more and more employees already had their own homes in the area and were brought out from Keswick by estate transport or came in their own cars.

Over a period of time, when two flats on the top floor of the house and a cottage at Derwent Bay became vacant, a new venture for Lingholm emerged in the establishment of self-catering accommodation, albeit in a small way. All three properties had spectacular views of Derwentwater and the surrounding fells, and gradually became more and more popular. Holidaymakers came from all over the country, with many repeat visits.

- - - - -

A most remarkable recollection came to light years later regarding a holiday visit to one of the flats on several occasions by a couple from London.

The Second World War and the years preceding it are still vividly remembered by many people in this country, but for young people today are now part of history. A very moving story from that time was of a young British businessman and humanitarian, Nicholas Winton. Following an earlier visit to Prague in 1938, and anticipating the threat to Jews in Nazi-occupied Czechoslovakia (as it then was), he managed to organise the evacuation of several hundred mainly Jewish children by train across Europe during the last months before the outbreak of war in September 1939 and to bring them to safety in England. A number of journeys were made, known as the 'Czech Kindertransport.' Among these children was a young boy aged six whose father had already escaped to England. His mother was fortunately able to follow later, and the boy grew up in Britain, becoming involved in public life.

In 1988 Sir Nicholas Winton, a special guest on the television programme 'That's Life,' was seated in the front row of the theatre when a large group of men and women survivors surprised him as they stood up around him. Years later he was featured in another TV programme when again he had a wonderful surprise as, unknown to him, a group of survivors and their descendants greeted him on stage.

They were led by a gentleman, recognised as the visitor who had spent holidays at Lingholm with his wife all those years later; he had been that young boy aged six who had escaped to safety in England.

Lord and Lady Rochdale celebrated their golden wedding in 1981, and on that occasion the staff gathered in the estate office to surprise them with special gifts. They reached their diamond anniversary in 1991, and the staff came together once again to present them with a gift and a beautifully decorated cake.

Royal events were also a time for celebration. The Rochdales had both attended the Coronation in 1953, and in 1977 they invited the staff to a summer supper party in honour of the Silver Jubilee.

For many years a Christmas party was held for Lingholm staff and their families in the drawing room (or Stone room as it was known) between Christmas and New Year. A large Norway spruce became the centrepiece of the party; as it was about ten feet tall it took some time to decorate.

Entertainment for the children was provided in the earlier years, and when the Rochdale grandchildren sometimes came for the Christmas holidays, they joined in. Everyone received a present from Lord and Lady Rochdale, and a combined staff gift was always presented to them.

It was always a happy occasion, when everyone felt to be part of one large 'family.' Sometimes, however, other commitments prevented people from attending the party, but it seemed an omen that, in 1992, every member of staff turned up; Lord Rochdale sadly passed away the following May.

*Dining room*

*Stone room*

*Christmas staff party 1984*

# CHAPTER FOUR

*Gardens: Early development – Visitors' route –*
*Progress through the years – Events and visits –*
*The Beatrix Potter connection*

On May 11th 1970 Enid Wilson, local author and ornithologist, daughter of George Abraham, Keswick, wrote in The Guardian's 'Country Diary:'

"There is a dearth of great gardens in this north-west corner of England – understandably, perhaps in mountainous country where the climate can be fickle and where the very scenery is apt to dwarf man's efforts, but this year there is a welcome change. Lingholm, on the west side of Derwentwater, has opened its gardens for the summer and while one could not call Lingholm 'great' (it has no pretentions and is far too natural for that) it has true quality and a beauty all of its own. The formal garden near the house is unremarkable (except for one special little enclosed garden with red camellias, a stone pool and low azaleas) but the basis of the rest is old woods from which the sound of water or wind is seldom absent. There are tall beeches, native Scots pines, and much natural regeneration all thickly interwoven with mature rhododendrons and azaleas. The leafy woodland floor suits this planting, some of the rhododendrons are as tall as small trees with rusty-backed leaves and shy white flowers; some have scarlet, waxy blooms and softly-peeling bark – indeed there is bewildering variety but my favourites are the yellow rhododendrons and a bush, which looks as if a flight of violet butterflies had settled among green leaves. There are many woodland birds and the bare beeches now house and reveal a thriving colony of herons – about thirty nests, where young are being fed. There is history here, too. Copper Heap Bay, where three centuries ago the Elizabethan miners dumped the copper ore from Newlands before rowing it to Keswick to smelt, is on the lake's edge where Beatrix Potter found her 'Squirrel Nutkin' who sailed to the island and nearly met his end there. 'Nutkins' still scold in the woods, but better than trees, birds or squirrels Lingholm offers something else – tranquillity in an untranquil world."

These last sentiments were what had prompted Lord Rochdale to open Lingholm gardens to the public in April 1970. Having enjoyed their visits to gardens all round the country, he and Lady Rochdale wanted to share the beauty and peace of their own garden with others.

But much change over the years had preceded all of the above. From early photographs it seemed that originally there were only lawns with a fringe of shrubs and trees around the house itself. Lord Rochdale's father had gradually developed the garden from the time of his arrival in the early 1900s, when stepped terraces along the lakeside of the house were built. Near the entrance gateway an attractive water garden, designed by Symons-Jeune, the well-known creator of natural rock gardening in the early twentieth century, was created in 1927, but has not survived.

On Lord Rochdale's return from war service and his arrival at Lingholm in 1946 to take over the estate, it was obvious that the garden had suffered understandably from neglect during the war. Gradually, with the establishment of a gardens department, progress continued. The terraces were altered into long gravel paths between grass borders and beds of seasonal plantings, including mixed shrubs and rhododendrons. A view from the lower terrace across a wide lawn – originally two tennis courts – towards colourful rhododendrons and maples gave glimpses of the lake. These original courts, built by Lord Rochdale's father, an accomplished tennis player from his Cambridge days, were kept in immaculate condition and were the venue for invitation tournaments, among guests being Suzanne Lenglen, legendary French Wimbledon champion of the 1920s.

In the grounds were the greenhouses, potting shed, kitchen garden and nursery. Not far away was a large barn that, during the early years of the gardens operation, housed a small livestock enterprise. A few pedigree Large White pigs, known as 'Swinside,' were introduced, with adjacent farrowing pens. A small flock of hens was housed on the upper floor of the barn, running free. After some years this enterprise, being small, inevitably had to cease. The house was kept supplied from the kitchen garden with vegetables, soft fruit and flowers, with any surplus being sold to local retailers. However, outside sales gradually ended with the opening of the gardens to the public. A small vinery in one of the greenhouses produced green muscatel grapes, but in later years the vines were no longer productive. As time passed, more and more varieties of plants and shrubs were introduced. The formal gardens blossomed with colour: rhododendrons (including miniatures), herbaceous borders, roses, begonias and Himalayan blue poppies, while ongoing new plants enhanced the woodland garden.

On leaving the car park, through the main gate and up the drive towards the gardens entrance, splashes of colour could be seen across the lawn and grass verges with a backcloth of magnificent large trees, including beech, cedar, silver fir and redwood (sequoiadendron Wellingtonia). Earlier, below the house, a group of laburnum trees decorated the triangular lawn. Years later these were infected by honey fungus and sadly had to be felled. Entering the formal garden, past a spectacular magnolia tree by the house, visitors would proceed via steps into a sunken memorial garden with a paved area round a central lily pond. Here there were mixed shrubs and plants, and a swathe of Japanese azaleas – a blaze of colour in the spring. And so through a gateway to the lower terrace with more plantings thriving below a sheltering high wall. Wheelchair visitors could avoid the steps and enter the garden along the top terrace, joining the main path at the end.

Continuing on through wrought iron gates round the south side of the house, stone walls covered in purple and yellow flowers, seasonal plantings including massed begonias, autumn gentians, lavender and blue poppies, would greet the visitor. Looking south towards Catbells and the Borrowdale fells, a gently sloping area of grass was spread with a carpet of daffodils in the spring, and later an avenue of cherry trees exploded with pink blossom. At the end of the formal garden was a colourful bank of Japanese evergreen azaleas, and a tall tree – a Chilean fire bush (embothrium coccineum) with bright red flowers – standing sentinel over them. When the tree later suffered gale damage it had to be felled.

From the formal garden, passing a varied collection of primulas, followed by groups of young camellias sheltered below a line of trees on the left, a narrow road took the visitor past a large bank of trees and shrubs. Here a gravel path wound up to give a better view across the orchard near massed azaleas, and beyond more colourful azaleas by an all-weather tennis court. Entering the woodland walk of about one mile the visitor would arrive at the main collection of azaleas and rhododendrons, many species and hybrids, with some rhododendrons as big as trees. The planting of this area started in the 1920s and 1930s. Lord Rochdale's father was a great friend of Sir John Ramsden, the then owner of Muncaster Castle, near Ravenglass, who had sponsored expeditions to China to collect rhododendron seedlings for his own garden. Some of these were planted at Lingholm and were the forerunners of the later collections. The central woodland area containing these became known at Lingholm as 'Muncaster valley.'

A circular route wound its way up through an avenue of rhododendrons and other shrubs and down a slope of gigantic beech trees and fine conifers underplanted with Himalayan blue poppies, to rejoin the main woodland path. For a number of years these trees housed a large heronry, a noisy area during the nesting season, and was of interest to members of the British Trust for Ornithology. When a few of these trees later suffered gale damage or disease and had to be felled, the herons departed and moved to another woodland in neighbouring Fawe Park.

During one season a young bird fell from its nest, survived, and found its way to the lawn in front of the house. 'Hubert,' as he was nicknamed, came regularly and used to stand stock still on the lawn, with the result that visitors, thinking him to be a statue, approached to take photographs, and then were startled when he moved!

Several small paths meandered away from the main walk to allow visitors to get closer to many of the plantings, and to view the magnificent specimen trees of interest, magnolias, beech, oak, sycamore, silver firs and other conifers. The intention at Lingholm, in caring for the woodland garden, was always to allow it to remain as natural as possible.

Although mainly a spring garden there was always something of interest for the visitor throughout the whole season from April to the end of October – cottage garden plants, late flowering scented rhododendrons and spectacular autumn colours, including Japanese maples. The house itself put on its own display with a brilliant red covering of Virginia creeper. On many occasions red squirrels could be seen scuttling up and down the house and on to window sills, sometimes jumping through an open bedroom window and leaving their 'calling card' in the occupant's bedroom slippers! With the arrival of more visitors to the gardens the squirrels gradually moved away and found sanctuary in the woods, even before the arrival of grey squirrels in the area.

Home propagation was an important part of the gardens enterprise, and a wide selection of plants and shrubs, many grown from seed or cuttings from Lingholm parent stock, were available for sale in the plant centre, which was open all year.

In 1985, with the help of a grant from the then English Tourist Board, a tea room, built by Lingholm maintenance department, was opened, offering morning coffee, light lunches and teas, all home-baked on the premises; Jenny's apple pie was scrumptious. The tea room enhanced a visit to the gardens, where visitors could enjoy welcome refreshments either inside or outside on the verandah or lawn below; it became popular with local residents as a meeting place. Occasionally, visitors would spend the whole day there, arriving for morning coffee, and having lunch and tea later, after spending further time in the gardens. It was staffed by a friendly team of ladies, sometime with extra student help and volunteers, especially on busy bank holidays. It was not unknown for the 'boss' himself to be seen in the kitchen with his sleeves rolled up, helping with the washing up! The tea room housed a small gift shop, where seeds from Lingholm stock could be bought, including varieties of the popular meconopsis (blue poppy).

It is appropriate here to recall the occasion when a visitor to the gardens called to make herself known to Lord Rochdale, who was fortunately at home at the time. It turned out she was the second wife of Frank Kingdon-Ward, the eminent plant hunter and botanist who travelled extensively in Asia in the early years of the twentieth century. He was one of the first botanists to bring back seeds of the distinctive Himalayan blue poppy. Meeting her was a most interesting interlude for Lord Rochdale in view of the connection with the origin of so many plants grown at Lingholm.

As the years passed Lingholm gardens became more well-known with increased publicity in magazines and tourist guides. Various authors, artists and photographers depicted the gardens in their books. Vivian Russell, former wife of the late Ken Russell, highlighted Lingholm in her 'Dream Gardens,' and Hunter Davies in his 'Good Guide to the Lakes' said of Lingholm it was "not to be missed." Several events during the 1980s brought the gardens to the attention of many more visitors.

In June 1981 a series of British Isles postage stamps were produced for the National Trust depicting iconic views from the four countries of the United Kingdom, with Derwentwater representing the English stamp. For the first day cover envelope, Lingholm was asked for a photograph taken in the gardens to promote the area. On June 24th, when the first day cover appeared, a 1920s Royal Mail van was parked at the front of the house, adding attraction to the occasion.

In July 1986 the Sunday Times colour magazine featured the gardens in an extended article by Graham Rose, the then gardening correspondent.

When the new head gardener and expert plantsman Mike Swift arrived in 1983, he brought new ideas as to how to further promote Lingholm. Among these was to persuade the BBC to showcase the gardens on Gardeners' World. The request was eventually granted in 1987, and it was very fortunate that the late Geoff Hamilton, and Roy Lancaster, traveller and plantsman, were both available to present the programme. Various aspects of planting in the woods and formal garden, and propagation in the greenhouses were demonstrated by Mike with help from Geoff. Lord Rochdale accompanied Roy Lancaster along the woodland walk to show him some of the special rhododendrons, and Roy remarked that he could have been on a Himalayan hillside; both also seemed undeterred by the rain falling at the time. Although filmed in early April, the first rhododendrons were in full bloom, and the magnificent carpet of daffodils near the house made a spectacular opening sequence.

Coach parties became popular, among which were specialist horticultural groups. One such was the American Horticultural Society of Virginia on a gardens cruise round the UK, docking at Workington to visit Cumbrian gardens. The president later wrote in appreciation of the warm welcome they received and the delight they experienced in the "vast collection of plants grouped so exquisitely together" and the "loving care each detail receives." Another came from the Rhododendron & Camellia Group of the Royal Horticultural Society, whose leader wrote afterwards that the garden was "so beautifully cared for, but managing to look natural." The leader of a party from a Field Study Centre in Wales, visiting in April 1988, later praised the care taken in the excellent identification of plants, the enthusiasm and genuine helpfulness of the head gardener and the welcome from the tea room staff.

In May 1992 Lingholm won the first prize for a new entrant in the Scottish Rhododendron Society's annual show in Glasgow. Special rhododendrons won a silver medal in April 1993 at the RHS Rhododendron Camellia & Magnolia show in London.

The first Holker Hall Garden & Countryside Festival, opened by the Duke of Edinburgh, took place in June 1992, and was the first of its kind in north-west England; Lingholm had a stand there. Sadly, this was to be the one and only time Lingholm could take part in this event, but fortunately Lord Rochdale was able to be there. A lady from Windermere, following a visit to the festival, decided to visit Lingholm. "Have visited many large gardens all over but this was one of the very best," she wrote. Another comment, made by a visitor who had picked up a leaflet in the Tourist Information Centre, was that Lingholm was "without doubt one of the best places to visit, both the gardens and the tea room, service all round second to none."

Like all gardens Lingholm suffered from extreme weather conditions. Notably, in early 1974 a near hurricane swept across the main woodland path, uprooting a huge Douglas fir. A good part of it was moved before the gardens opened that year, but the path had to be diverted for the season. In 1976, well remembered for its summer drought, household and bath water had to be collected in small tanks and taken by tractor and trailer into the woods, and transferred into plastic containers with holes drilled in the bottom, strategically placed by rhododendrons and azaleas most at risk.

Other freak weather events included an extremely hard frost one late April, which caught most of the rhododendrons; notices had to be hurriedly put up to warn visitors. Another occasion was a sudden snowfall one day in early June followed by the start of a heatwave four days later.

In May 1993 Mike Swift was invited by his friend Kenneth Cox, head gardener at Glendoick Gardens, Perth, to join a party of gardeners he was leading on a visit to China. This was a great opportunity to study rhododendrons and other plants in their native habitat, on a three-week trek in western China. Lord Rochdale was delighted for Mike to join the group, and although he received news from him of his first days in China, it was sad that he had passed away before Mike returned and could tell him of his exploits.

Many gardens throughout the country open to the public one or two days a year on behalf of the National Gardens Scheme, raising money for charities. Lord Rochdale's father was a founder member of the scheme in 1927, with Lingholm supporting both the National Gardens Scheme and the Gardeners' Benevolent Society. In honour of the Diamond Jubilee of the NGS in 1987, an ornamental Indian horse chestnut tree from the north-west Himalayas was presented to Lingholm and planted near the orchard. Following Lord Rochdale's death, later in 1993 a long-service award was made to Lingholm for over sixty years' support, and Elinor, Viscountess Rochdale received a presentation garden hand fork to mark the event.

Throughout his life at Lingholm the gardens were Lord Rochdale's main hobby and, indeed, his passion. On returning home after a busy life away he liked nothing better than spending time at weekends working somewhere in his woodland garden enjoying the peace and relaxation it offered. Visitors would see him in his old clothes and sometimes mistook him for one of his gardeners!

When he retired from his business life he would spend more time working in the gardens, Elinor joining in on occasions; there was also welcome additional help from some Lingholm residents. As with all gardens, however, the work was never-ending but ever satisfying.

Many books have been written about Beatrix Potter, but some people may not know that as a young woman approaching thirty she and her family stayed at Lingholm as their summer residence for several years in the late 1890s and early 1900s. Following earlier holidays in Scotland and at Wray Castle near Hawkshead, they came to Lingholm. It was here that Beatrix wandered through the woods, finding further inspiration for her artistic talents, using many sketches as background for her little animal stories.

*Beatrix Potter and brother Bertram at Lingholm*

During this time she wrote her Tale of Squirrel Nutkin, and her sketch of St. Herbert's Island from the lakeshore at Lingholm was the basis for Owl Island in the story. While at Lingholm she also spent time walking in Newlands valley, sketching views that would later be used for her Tale of Mrs. Tiggy-Winkle; the farm at Skelgill was also featured as Lucie's home.

Beatrix's artistic talents varied greatly: animals, fungi, landscapes and interiors. In the 'Art of Beatrix Potter' is a painting of the hallway and main staircase at Lingholm, as well as interiors at neighbouring Fawe Park where she stayed later with her family. There she wrote the Tale of Benjamin Bunny, and the kitchen garden became Mr. McGregor's garden.

Rupert Potter, Beatrix's father, was a keen photographer and took many photographs while at Lingholm. A number of these were found many years later at Castle Cottage, Sawrey, Beatrix's home after her marriage to William Heelis, and later owned by the National Trust. The tenant living there, a National Trust committee member who knew the Rochdales, handed them over to Lord Rochdale for safekeeping, and to provide an appropriate home for them.

In 1988 the BBC was making a film of Beatrix Potter's life in two parts, and asked permission to film at Lingholm, travelling through the Lake District from Wray Castle, her earlier holiday home in Cumbria. Hunter Davies accompanied the BBC producer, recounting to him her life story. The first part concluded in Beatrix Potter's home at Hill Top, Sawrey, where they browsed amongst her books and memorabilia in the gift shop and talked to visitors. The second part was about her life after marriage, and as a sheep farmer. At Lingholm they met the Rochdales and saw the surroundings Beatrix knew so well, and Rupert Potter's photographs were produced to recall those earlier days. Their two Pekinese dogs, present during the filming, would have been quite at home with Beatrix when she was confined to the house in her last months, as she said her own two pekes were 'great company' and her 'most efficient footwarmers'!

Her little books are now a worldwide success, with outlets selling merchandise based on her animal characters, and which she called her 'little side shows.' However, in the early days of her writing, and longing for financial independence, she persuaded a publisher to produce greeting cards depicting her animal drawings. With this small success she was earning a little money for herself, and so it could be said that, during her lifetime, she had initiated the commercialism that surrounds her name today. In fact she once remarked 'I think I have little friends all over the world.' Her tales are now available in forty languages, with recent additions, as recorded in 2011, being Mandarin Chinese, Lithuanian, and Lowland Scots! A new edition of the Tale of Peter Rabbit had appeared in the Scottish dialect in 2004.

Beatrix would also have been gratified that in 1980, nearly forty years after her death, the Beatrix Potter Society was founded by a group of people who were professionally involved in the curatorship of her material. Its aims were to promote the study and appreciation of her as an author of children's literature, natural history and landscape artist, diarist, farmer, conservationist, and owner of 4000 acres of land in the Lake District which she gifted to the National Trust. The Society continues to thrive, holding meetings and social events nationwide and abroad; it produces members' quarterly newsletters, reporting events in the UK and overseas, from as far away as Russia, Korea, Japan and Australia. A biennial International Study Conference is held in July based in the Lake District or Scotland, with tours to various places connected with Beatrix.

Delegates to the inaugural conference in 1984, based in Ambleside, came to Lingholm and the Newlands valley, and were entertained to morning coffee in Lingholm. A later occasion was in 1988 when, by chance, the visit coincided with the filming by the BBC mentioned earlier. During filming outside the house, Society members were walking into the gardens when Hunter Davies saw the party arrive and had a brief conversation with a few of them, most being from America, but also Japan and, of course, the UK. In the group was Brigadier John Heelis, great-nephew of William Heelis, who had a chat, expressing his amazement at Beatrix's ongoing worldwide success. This episode added further interest, before the BBC left to continue filming in the south Lakes at Hill Top, Sawrey.

Beatrix Potter has a huge following throughout America. Coach parties of American visitors came to Lingholm as part of 'whistle-stop' literary tours round Britain. It is also well known that the Japanese are devoted to her little tales, and follow her life avidly, even making their own television films about her and Lingholm.

On one occasion the office door bell rang, and there stood a Japanese gentleman, who very courteously announced the arrival of his party at the nearby garden entrance. He said he was a professor of children's literature at a Japanese university, and his party were each clutching a copy of 'Squirrel Nutkin' in Japanese. Another occasion was when a Japanese family were seen taking photographs of their figurine of Jeremy Fisher, placed carefully beside the lily pond in the memorial garden!

Beatrix Potter's holiday home beside Derwentwater has certainly added great interest for many visitors to the gardens, and to the story of Lingholm itself.

*French Horticultural Society visit 1973*

*First Day Cover 24th June 1981*

*Post Office vintage van, front of house*

*"Hubert" the heron on front lawn*

*Red squirrel*

# CHAPTER FIVE

*Some early personal memories –*
*Memories of final years 1993 - 1997*
*Conclusion*

In coming to the end of this story a final chapter has yet to unfold, where some of my personal memories appear, and when the estate departments were gradually closing down.

I had returned to the UK in late September 1962 on my final leave after five years working in Northern Nigeria, at a time when the world was holding its breath in the shadow of the Cuban missile crisis, and an uncertain future. While on leave I answered an advertisement for a personal secretary to Lord Rochdale on his country estate near Keswick, to start in early January 1963 – and the rest is history.

The winter of 1962/63 was one of the coldest and longest of the twentieth century. Derwentwater was frozen solid to a depth of eighteen inches, but for several weeks there were cloudless skies and unbroken sunshine. One of the earliest memories of my new surroundings was of walking across the frozen lake from Lingholm to the Keswick boat landings, climbing Castlehead and looking down on Derwentwater where the ice shone pink in the setting sun – it was quite magical. My introduction to the estate as a whole was when I was accompanied up Swinside fell for an excellent bird's eye view from the top of all the estate land and properties in Newlands valley.

From the estate office window the view east across the terraced garden gave glimpses of Derwentwater through the trees, with the Borrowdale fells in the background. I felt very fortunate to be living and working in such a beautiful place.

My working life, as many readers will have experienced, was so different from that of today. In 1963 the telephone was still operator controlled: Lingholm's number was Keswick 3, police station Keswick 4, I believe Lodore Hotel was Keswick 2, but I never found out who was Keswick 1! There were no computers, mobile phones, fax machines or even calculators; all records were kept in filing cabinets. Life was just as busy as today, but lived at a slower pace – the new technologies were still a long way off.

Throughout the ensuing years, as in all businesses, I had to adapt to new office procedures. Decimalisation and VAT were introduced in the 1970s. In the early part of that decade during industrial action and a three-day working week, postal strikes and power cuts caused disruption, but a threatened long-running petrol shortage fortunately never materialised. I remember we had to be prepared and received petrol coupons for both business and private use – I still have my allocation. During this time a local garage displayed scooters for sale as an alternative means of private transport to save petrol.

Later, as computers were being introduced, working on my own I did not wish to alter what was working well for the estate and myself; I had already adapted to streamlined banking, fax machine and electric typewriter. As retirement approached, although I could have changed by then to a computerised office system, I did not wish to do so at that stage; what an upheaval it would have been for all concerned . . . not least myself!

On completing 30 years at Lingholm in January 1993, I invited the staff to an informal party with an invitation in the form of a fun 'confidential office memo,' asking them to help me celebrate "30 years' hard labour." They responded by giving me an imitation pickaxe from the 'Chain gang'! This occasion was the last time the staff and Lord and Lady Rochdale gathered together at Lingholm.

*Lord Rochdale*

Lord Rochdale passed away peacefully at home on 24th May, 1993, and my world as I had known it for the past 30 years came to an abrupt end. Life, however, had to go on, but an inherited estate nearly always involves change, and much work still had to be done.

At his funeral at Carlisle crematorium, family, estate staff, friends and colleagues came to pay their respects and say farewell in a simple Christian Science service.

As his father before him Lord Rochdale had expressed a wish that a thanksgiving service be held at Parliament's Church, St. Margaret's, Westminster Abbey, so that his many friends and colleagues from further afield could gather together to celebrate his life; this was arranged for 29th September, 1993.

Planning for this event took some time, initiated by the clergy at St. Margaret's Church in conjunction with the family. I was very much involved, with the office fax machine in constant use for sending and receiving details of the service; I found the preparations for this special day a most interesting experience.

I travelled to London in July with Lord Rochdale's son, St. John, the new Viscount, to meet the clergy and administrative staff of St. Margaret's for discussions as the normal prerequisite for holding the service there. As the parliament buildings were only a short walk across the road I was able to meet the catering manageress at the House of Lords to arrange the buffet refreshments following the service, and for the florist to provide displays in the church.

The hour-long service in September began exactly as Big Ben struck noon, when the choir sang the first note of the Introit. The Reverend Dr. Donald Gray, rector of St. Margaret's (also Chaplain to the Speaker of the House of Commons) officiated at the service, assisted by the Reverend Rodney Hughes, Vicar of Crosthwaite Church, Keswick, who led the prayers. A most moving address was given by the former Lord Bishop of Carlisle, the Right Reverend David Halsey; he and his wife were good friends of the Rochdales.

Following the service one of the clergy whom I had met in July told me it was the finest address he had heard at such a service, and that Lord Rochdale must have been the kindest of men, held in great affection and esteem.

One of Lord Rochdale's great interests was music, he and Elinor regularly attending concerts at Rosehill Theatre, near Whitehaven. His friend Sir Nicholas Sekers, founder of the theatre, had invited him to become Chairman of Trustees in 1970, and having helped to steer the theatre through difficult times, he retired in 1983.

In May 1994 Rosehill trustees wished to remember Lord Rochdale in a memorial concert. His great-niece Sacha Barlow, an accomplished violinist whose career he had followed with great interest, joined in a duo with Cumbrian pianist Michael Hancock to give a memorable recital. Many friends met together to support Elinor Rochdale on that occasion.

During the months that followed Lord Rochdale's death, work focussed on matters of his personal estate, and I completed my work for the estate company by the middle of 1994. By that time the staff knew that changes were bound to come. The gardens, however, remained open and I continued working for the department until I finished in February 1995 and in May went to live in Keswick.

Elinor Rochdale had always hoped the gardens would continue to thrive as a tribute to the many years of hard work by the gardens staff, for its well-known reputation both locally and nationally, and especially as it had been such an integral part of her husband's and her life at Lingholm. I continued on a part-time basis helping Elinor both at Lingholm and after she had moved into The Lodge at Lingholm. I worked for her there until she sadly passed away in January 1997, and I finally left Lingholm in May of that year, after thirty-four years.

During the writing of this book Lingholm house and surrounding cottages and grounds were sold to new owners, but the estate farms, forestry plantations and woodland garden remain in the ownership of the Rochdale family.

What happened to the house and estate staff who had remained after 1993?

Maureen and Tony Jones had hoped to remain at Lingholm permanently with Lady Rochdale, but in 1994 they were unexpectedly recalled to New Zealand. New help was then urgently required; Shelagh and Barry Keeton from Yorkshire were taken on, remaining until 1997. Ann Payne, the only remaining part-time member of the house staff, had worked for Lady Rochdale for more than ten years, and left in 1994 to live in America.

The head gardener Mike Swift, and his German assistant Cornelia Rapp had decided to leave towards the end of 1994. Mike became head gardener at Torosay Castle and Gardens on the idyllic Isle of Mull, while Cornelia went to work in the renowned gardens at Sissinghurst Castle in Kent, the creation of Vita Sackville-West and her husband Harold Nicholson.

When the forestry department closed about this time, head forester

Ronnie Pepper and his son Anthony, who had worked with his father, also left Lingholm. They became self-employed, later worked together, and some years ago were responsible for the felling of trees and opening up the shore alongside Thirlmere beside the A591.

Forester Simon Willan remained at Derwent Bay, leased the Lingholm forestry premises, and with a partner started up a wood carving business called 'Derwent Bay Bears,' together with a shop selling mainly wooden gifts. As the business developed, bears of all sizes, and later other animals, were made and displayed for sale. Their popularity spread and they were sold nationwide and abroad. Later, Simon started displaying his work at various country estate shows; this has now ceased owing to his increasing workload in Cumbria. On the expiry of his lease some years ago, he relocated his business to near Penrith under the name 'Cumbrian Bears.'

Maintenance foreman Terry Wood left Lingholm in March 1995 to live and work in Lancashire.

After Elinor Rochdale passed away, the regrettable decision was made to close the gardens and tearoom. A new head gardener, appointed in early 1995, left for a similar appointment on a country estate in the Scottish borders. Peter Rainey, a Keswick man, had joined the department in 1989 and trained under Mike Swift with day release at Newton Rigg College. On leaving Lingholm in 1997 he continued a varied career locally, including taking a degree in Turf Management at Myerscough College, University of Central Lancashire, where he won Student of the Year Award. Today he is locally in great demand as a self-employed experienced gardener.

Of the six tearoom ladies, two continued in the catering business, and I understand the other four did not pursue further work.

I must record here the progress of an earlier trainee in the gardens department. Janet Cubey, a Lorton girl and former pupil of Keswick School, always had a passion for horticulture and came to Lingholm about 1990 for pre-college practical training, including attending Newton Rigg College. She went on to train at the Royal Botanic Garden, Edinburgh, followed by work at Ness Botanic Garden attached to Liverpool University, where she met her future husband Wolfgang Bopp, from Germany. He was later appointed curator of the new National Botanic Garden of Wales, Carmarthenshire, where Janet worked for a while before taking up a post in 1999 as botanist at the Royal Horticultural Society's garden at Wisley.

Today they live in Hampshire, Janet working as a senior botanist at Wisley, currently developing the botanical and horticultural content of the Society's databases. She is also Editor-in-Chief of its annual RHS Plant Magazine (a full-time job in itself) while Wolfgang is Director of the Sir Harold Hillier Garden and Arboretum, Romsey.

Janet often travels abroad in the course of her work, and in the past has been on three plant expeditions to China. Her keenness as a student gained her a place on the first with Mike Swift in Kenneth Cox's party in 1993. Since then she was invited by Kenneth Cox to join a second one, followed by a third expedition, led by herself.

Her love and enthusiasm for plants and horticulture has carried her through into a successful career, and it all started at Lingholm.

Whilst writing this book, I found a news item taking us back to the earliest days when Lingholm was the country retreat of Colonel Greenall whose land was divided into three small estates. The Keswick Lakes Visitor & Keswick Guardian of 1886, kept in the Keswick Museum & Art Gallery archives, and mentioned in the Keswick Reminder in 2011, referred to a sale by auction in London of three local estates – Lingholm, Derwent Bay and Swinside.

The contrast between life in Victorian London and the beauty of this corner of north-west England must have had a profound effect on the auctioneer. In his opening remarks at the sale, he said that Lingholm was the loveliest place on which he had ever cast eyes; it was most entrancing, the glorious scenery being beyond all description. He never saw a more beautiful place in his life.

Lingholm's name will always live on in one of its most beautiful plants, the Himalayan blue poppy. Mike Swift had been developing a new hybrid over a number of years from parent plants, seeds of which were sold regularly in the plant centre. However, not until later did the new name finally appear in various gardens, seen both by myself and others.

*Meconopsis "Lingholm"*

Meconopsis 'Lingholm' is a sturdy perennial with large, deep sky blue flowers and is quoted as being the most beautiful of the Meconopsis group. 'Lingholm' plants and seeds are sold to the public and trade all over the UK and to countries far and wide.

In conclusion: Lingholm gardens were always part of a larger estate, as described earlier. But the gardens are what has defined Lingholm in the hearts of all those who visited them over many years, and for whom their closure in 1997 was a great loss.

This prompted the inspiration for the following poem written by my sister. Knowing Lingholm well, she illustrates in a charming word-picture images of what delighted everyone, and not least myself.

## ENCHANTED GARDEN
### by Joan Corney

There are shadows in the woods,
Amongst the rhododendrons
That crowd a woodland path
Or clamber up the slopes.
Amongst azaleas pink and gold,
Beneath the towering pines,
Under beeches rising high.
They watch a squirrel scampering
From tree to tree.

They follow the steps of a young fox
Slowly treading a woodland path.
They sit and look at the hills
And listen to the peace and stillness
Where only the song of the birds
Can be heard.

There are shadows by the fruit-trees
Where in spring a carpet of gold
Lies spread beneath.
Amongst a mosaic of colours
Mingling with moss and grey stone.
There are shadows by the shore
Where the woodland meets the lake
With the gentle ripple of the surface
By the water's edge.

Through many years these shadows
All have passed their way,
But they are shadows of happiness,
Echoes of the peace and joy
That Nature and the hands of love
Gave to this enchanted place.

And so I bring my memories and story of Lingholm to a close, the writing of which has been for me a labour of love.

# POSTSCRIPT

Since writing my book, the family sadness of recent months has brought back a memory for me of St. John's children who, in the 1970s, spent happy holidays with their grandparents at Lingholm. Now, years later they and I have met again, and we have come full circle, with a happy link to the past for all of us.

# BIOGRAPHY

*Marjorie Dymock*

Marjorie Dymock was born of Scottish parents, brought up in Bolton, Lancashire, and trained as a private secretary. After first working for six years near Manchester and then as PA for five years with the Government of Northern Nigeria, she returned to the UK in late 1962. She then became personal secretary to the 1st Viscount Rochdale on his country estate near Keswick from January 1963 for the next 34 years, retiring in 1997; she has remained in Keswick since retirement. After the closure of Lingholm as a working estate, and also the much-loved gardens, she had wished to write its story, including Lord Rochdale's life – he had never wanted to write his memoirs. With the hope that Lingholm should never be forgotten for what it had been for so many years, in a concise and readable book that wish has now been fulfilled.